MW01691999

Simple Machines

CONTENTS

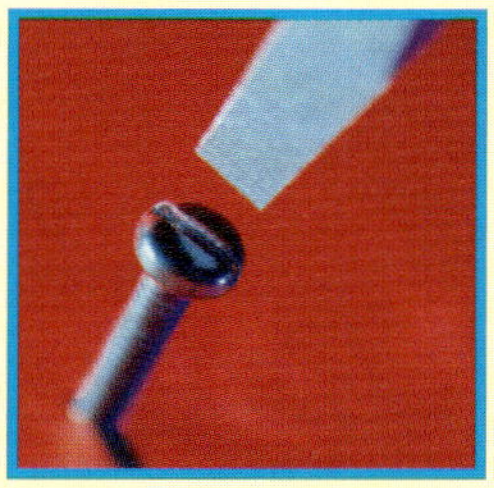

Think About . . .

People in Science

Did You Know?

Think About . . .

What Makes Things Move?

If you look around, you'll see all kinds of moving things—from cars and trains to leaves on trees. But what makes some things move while other things stand still? A force is needed to make an object move. A **force** is a push or a pull. A force is also needed to make a moving object slow down, change direction, or stop moving. If you drop a ball, it falls to the ground. **Gravity,** the force that pulls objects toward the center of Earth, is acting on the ball. The unit used to measure force is called the **newton.**

About 300 years ago Sir Isaac Newton wrote that a moving object will keep moving unless a force acts on it. A ball rolling on a rug will slow down and stop because of friction. **Friction** is a force caused by one object rubbing against another. Friction between the ball and the rug slows and stops the ball.

Newton discovered that a still object will remain still unless a force acts on it. A ball sitting on a level floor will not start to move unless you push it. The tendency of an object to stay in motion or to stay still is called **inertia.**

Some objects move faster than others. The **speed** of an object tells how fast it is moving. Speed is usually described in terms of how far the object moves each second, minute, or hour.

A force can be a push or a pull. To make a wagon move, you can pull it or you can push it from behind.

How Are Work and Energy Related?

Suppose you push a shopping cart a certain distance through a store. Then, suppose a friend pushes on a wall with all his strength, but the wall does not move. Who is doing work? Scientists say that **work** is done only when a force makes something move. So pushing the grocery cart is work because the cart moves. Pushing on the wall is not work because the wall does not move.

To calculate work, you need to know how much force was applied to an object and the **distance** the object moved (Work = Force x distance). Work is measured in **joules.**

When scientists talk about **energy,** they are talking about the ability to do work. Anything that does work uses energy.

Things that are moving, such as a runner, have energy of **motion**—or **kinetic energy.** The faster something moves, the more kinetic energy it has.

If you are on a swing moving forward and up, you have kinetic energy. But when you reach the highest point in your swing, you stop for an instant. For that instant, you have no kinetic energy. All your energy is **potential energy,** which is stored energy. Your potential energy came from your kinetic energy. As you start to swing back down, your potential energy is changed back to kinetic energy. As you swing, you always have the same amount of energy. It just changes back and forth between kinetic and potential energy.

A girl pushes with a force of 5 newtons and moves the cart a distance of 2 meters. The work she has done is 5 newtons x 2 meters, or 10 joules.

What Are Simple Machines?

*A **machine** is any tool that makes it easier to do work. Some machines, like a car, are very complicated. Others are **simple machines** that usually have only one or two parts. The six types of simple machines are inclined plane, lever, wheel and axle, pulley, wedge, and screw. These machines are useful because they let us do more work than we could with just muscle power.*

Inclined Plane

An **inclined plane** is a flat surface with one end higher than the other. You can use an inclined plane to gradually raise or lower objects. A wheelchair ramp into a building and a road up a mountain are both inclined planes.

Suppose a mover uses an inclined plane to raise a heavy object. The mover does the same amount of work whether he lifts the object or pushes it up a ramp. Using a ramp, the mover must move the object a greater distance. But the ramp decreases the amount of force needed to raise the object. With a longer ramp, the mover would need even less force to move the object. But he would move it an even greater distance.

Friction always wastes some of the energy put into a machine. The **efficiency** of a machine compares how much work you get out of a machine with how much energy you put in. The efficiency of an inclined plane depends on its surface and the surface of the object being moved. If both surfaces are smooth, less energy is lost to friction. So the inclined plane's efficiency is high. If both surfaces are rough, the inclined plane's efficiency is low.

By using an inclined plane, the worker can use less force, but he must move the plant a greater distance.

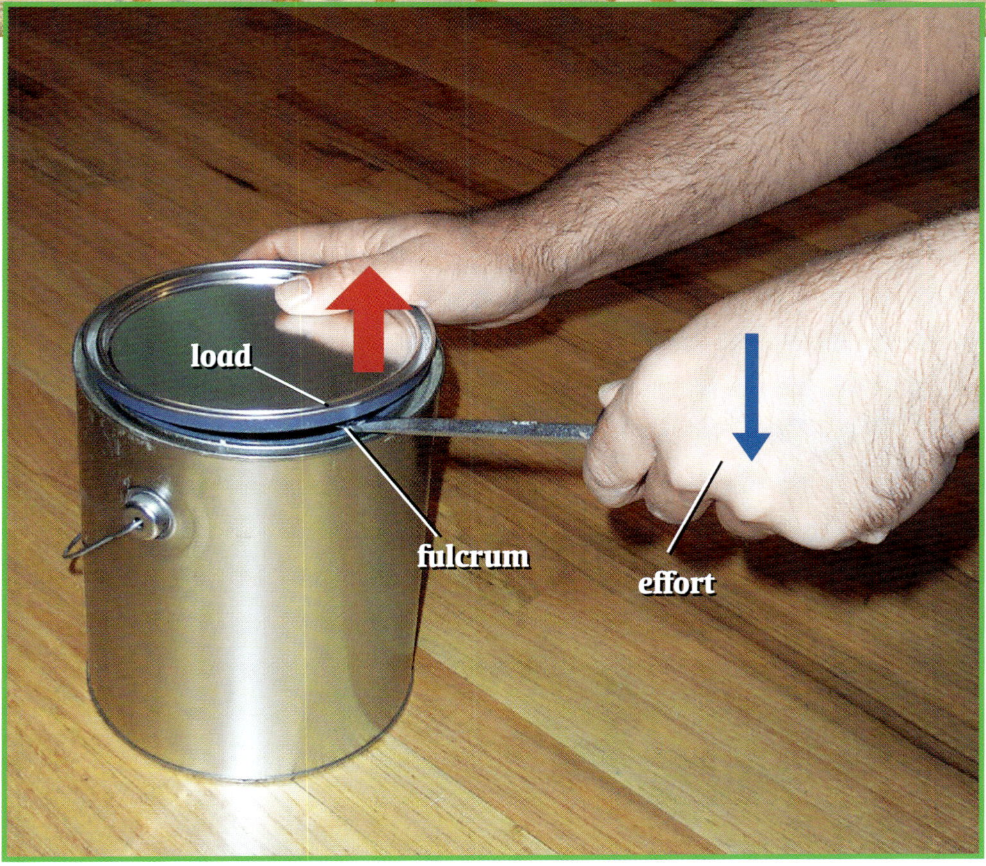

This screwdriver is used as a first-class lever. You push down on its handle to pry the lid of the can up.

Lever

Levers are machines that do work by turning around a fixed point. The point at which the bar of a lever pivots, or turns, is called the **fulcrum.** The force you apply to a lever is called the **effort.** The distance from the fulcrum to the effort is called the effort arm length. The **resistance** is the force exerted by the load you are trying to move. The distance from the fulcrum to the resistance is the resistance arm length. The closer the resistance is to the fulcrum, the less effort is needed to move the resistance.

Levers can be divided into three classes. They depend on the positions of the fulcrum, effort, and resistance. In first-class levers the fulcrum is located between the effort and the resistance. The effort and resistance move in opposite directions. Seesaws, scissors, and pliers are first-class levers.

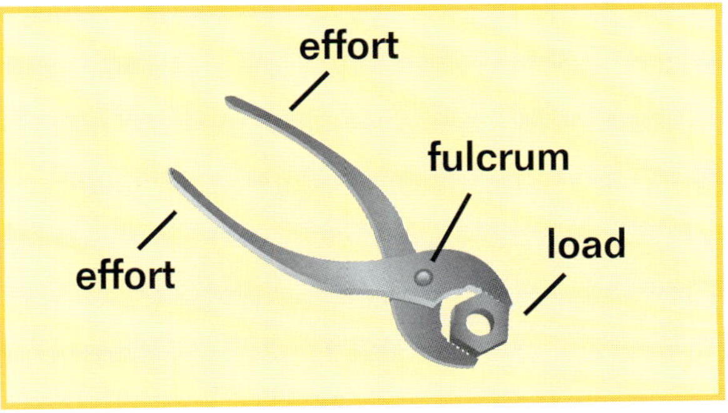

Pliers and scissors are double first-class levers. Effort is applied in two places.

In second-class levers the resistance is between the effort and the fulcrum. The fulcrum is often closer to the resistance. This kind of lever produces a gain in force. Nutcrackers and wheelbarrows are second-class levers.

In second-class levers the resistance moves in the same direction as the effort.

In third-class levers the effort is between the fulcrum and the resistance. This kind of lever usually produces a loss in force, but a gain in speed and distance. Brooms and fishing poles are third-class levers.

In third-class levers the resistance arm is longer than the effort arm.

You can read more about levers on page 14.

Wheel and Axle

A **wheel and axle** consists of a large wheel fixed to a smaller wheel or shaft called the axle. The two turn together. The effort is usually applied to the larger wheel. A small effort applied to the wheel will move a larger resistance on the axle.

A wheel and axle is a kind of lever that rotates in a circle around a center fulcrum. The larger wheel rotates around the smaller wheel (axle).

Think about the steering wheel on a car. The steering wheel and its column, which is the axle, turn together. As the wheel and axle turn together, a point on the wheel moves farther than a point on the axle. In return, the force exerted by the axle is greater than the force applied to the wheel. A wheel and axle lets you use less force to do work.

The larger the wheel is compared to the axle, the less force you have to apply. A wrench turning a nut, a steering wheel and column, and a faucet handle are all wheel-and-axle systems.

Examples of a fixed pulley system (left) and a fixed pulley paired with a movable pulley (right).

Pulley

A **pulley** is a kind of wheel with a groove. The groove allows a rope or cable to ride on the wheel without slipping off. A fixed pulley is attached to one spot and can be used to move a load up, down, or sideways. This type of pulley changes the direction of your force, but it does not reduce the amount of effort you have to use. Often a flagpole has a fixed pulley.

A movable pulley moves with the load along the rope. This type of pulley reduces the amount of effort you have to use, but it increases the distance you must pull the rope. A movable pulley does not change the direction of your force.

Movable pulleys are often combined with fixed pulleys. A group of pulleys, called a compound pulley, can be used to lift a very heavy object like a boat or piano. Compound pulleys can both change the direction of the force and reduce the amount of effort you have to use.

Wedge

A **wedge** is a simple machine that is really a type of inclined plane. A wedge can have either one or two sloping sides. A force is applied to the wide end of a wedge. The narrow end of the wedge is driven into an object. The sides of the wedge push the object apart.

The head of an axe has two sloping sides that meet at a sharp edge. People can use axes to split apart logs. The sides of other wedges, such as needles and nails, meet at a sharp point. Some tools, such as letter openers and chisels, are very narrow wedges. If you look at the blade of a saw, you will see that it is a row of tiny wedges. All these tools are used to cut into objects.

With any wedge, the sharper the edge or point, the less force that is needed to split or cut something. For example, if a saw blade is dull, it is much harder to cut through wood.

Screw

A **screw** is an inclined plane that is wrapped around a rod. When you turn a screw, the direction of your force is changed and increased. The closer the threads are, the less force you need to apply. People often use screws to hold wood or metal pieces together. A propeller and the threaded base of a light bulb are also screws.

A wood carver uses a wedge called a chisel to cut off small pieces of wood.

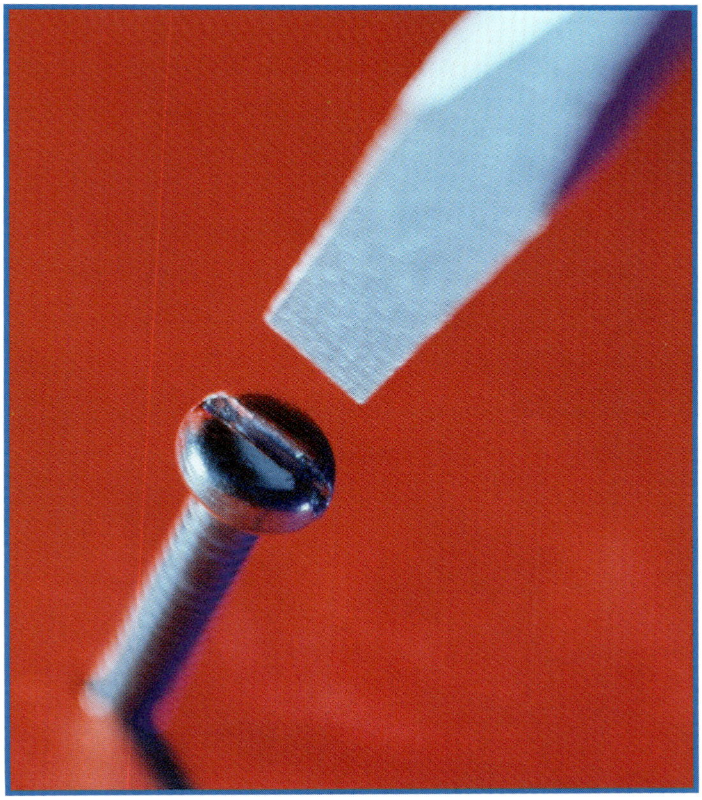

When you turn a screw into a surface, the threads wind their way into the surface and grip it with great strength.

What Are Compound Machines?

A **compound machine** is made of two or more simple machines. A pencil sharpener is a compound machine that contains levers, wheels and axles, screws, and wedges. Other compound machines, such as bicycles, roller coasters, and Ferris wheels, are made of many simple machines.

A Bicycle

The pedals and pedal sprocket are a **wheel-and-axle** system. Pedal one turn and the pedal sprocket goes around one time.

The chain is a kind of **pulley**. The chain transfers the motion of the pedal sprocket to one of the gears at the rear wheel.

Levers on the handlebars allow the brake cables to be pulled with a lot of force. The brake pads then press tightly against the wheel rims. The friction between the brake pads and wheel rims slows or stops the bicycle.

The handlebars on a bike are like the steering wheel of a car. They change the direction of motion. Both are **wheel-and-axle** systems. Put a force on the handlebar and motion is transferred to the axle.

The front wheel is a wheel with an axle. But the force you give to the pedals to move a bike forward is all applied to the rear wheel. No effort is directly applied to move the front wheel itself forward. The front wheel reduces friction as the bike moves along the ground.

A Combine

This amazing compound machine performs several jobs at once. It cuts and collects wheat in the field. Then it shakes the wheat until the grain drops off the stalk (straw). The machine separates the grain from the straw and moves the grain into a storage tank. The straw comes out of the back of the machine. The straw is left in rows in the field to be collected later.

Archimedes (287–212 B.C.E.)

Archimedes was a Greek scientist and mathematician. He was born in Sicily and went to school in Alexandria, Egypt. Archimedes spent most of his life doing research and experiments. One of the things he discovered was how a lever works. He supposedly said, "Give me a place to stand and a lever long enough, and I will move the Earth." Archimedes also invented the compound pulley.

While in Egypt, he invented a machine used for raising water from a lower to a higher level. The machine is known as the Archimedes screw.

The machine is a hollow cylinder that has a screw inside, which forms a spiral chamber. A handle at the top is used to turn the screw. By placing the lower end in water and turning the screw, water is raised to the top where it flows out an opening. This type of pump was used for irrigating farm fields and for draining areas of water.

The first screw pumps were powered by people or animals. Later some were powered by windmills. Today they are powered by electric or gasoline motors, and they are used in some wastewater plants. In addition to moving water, they are used to lift ashes, grain, sand, and other light materials.

When the handle was turned, water was lifted up inside the cylinder by the screw.

Lillian Gilbreth (1878–1972)

Lillian Gilbreth was a member of the National Women's Hall of Fame. She also became the first woman member of the National Academy of Engineering.

Have you ever used a trash can with a step-on lever that opens the lid of the can? If so, you've used one of the inventions of Lillian Moller Gilbreth.

Lillian Evelyn Moller grew up in a large family in Oakland, California. She graduated from the University of California and earned her doctorate from Brown University. In 1904 Lillian married Frank Gilbreth. He was interested in studying workers as they performed their tasks. Working together, the Gilbreths studied motion and ways to make workers more efficient. In 1924 Frank died suddenly. Dr. Lillian Gilbreth was left with their company and their twelve children.

Dr. Gilbreth was very successful in running the company. She suggested many ways for other companies to improve the way workers did their jobs. She also worked on improving the efficiency of household items. In addition to the trash can, she invented an electric food mixer and designed a kitchen that made work easier.

Dr. Gilbreth continued working until she was in her 80s. Two of her children wrote a book about the Gilbreth family's life. *Cheaper by the Dozen* tells about the humorous adventures of their large family.

Did You Know?

Your Body Has Levers

Your body's levers are made of bone and muscle systems that allow your body to move. If you sit in an upright position and completely relax your neck, your head will tip. This is because your neck muscles supply the force needed to hold your head up. The weight of your head is the resistance force. The fulcrum is located in the bones in your neck. In this case raising your head back up is an example of a first-class lever.

Your foot can also act as a lever. Try standing on the floor, then lift your heels off the floor to stand on your toes. When you do this, the resistance is your body weight pushing down. Muscles in your foot and the calf of your leg supply the effort force. The fulcrum is located at the joints where your toes connect to your foot bones. Since the resistance is between the effort and the fulcrum, your foot acts as a second-class lever.

You use your arm as a lever when you swing a bat, hammer a nail, or lift a spoonful of soup to your mouth. Try holding a book or a ball in one hand with your arm at your side. The palm of your hand should face forward. Keeping your upper arm still, bend your elbow and raise the book as high as your chest. Weightlifters call this lift a curl.

When you lift the book, the book is the load, or resistance. Your elbow joint is the fulcrum, and the biceps muscle in your upper arm provides the effort force. When you use your arm in the curl, it acts as a third-class lever.

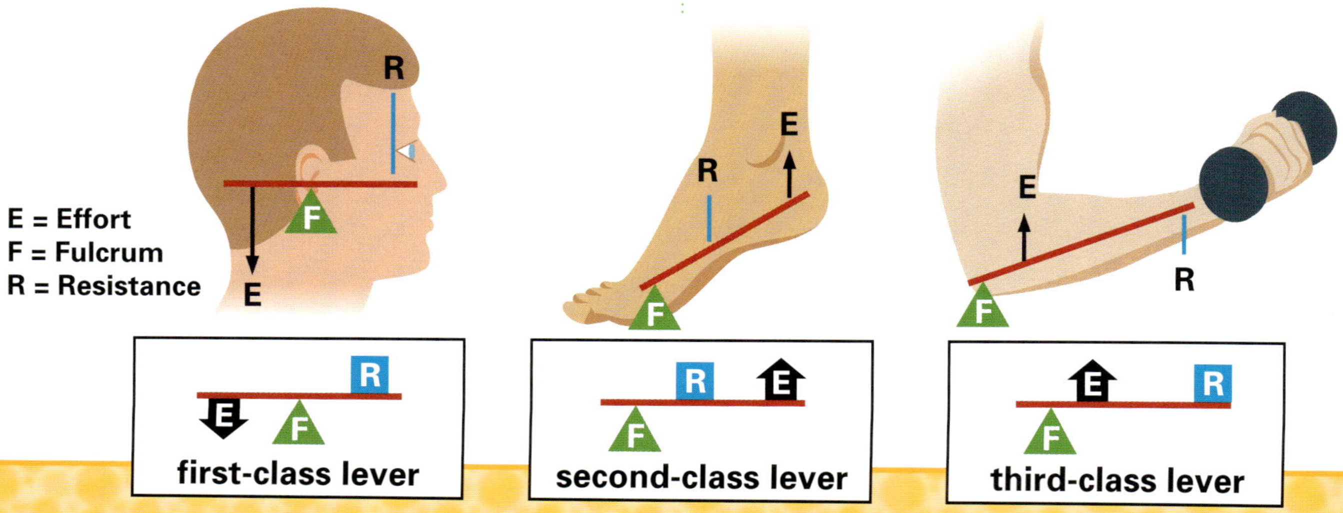

A roller coaster has no engine. It keeps moving because of gravity and inertia.

How a Roller Coaster Works

Have you ever ridden a roller coaster? A roller coaster track is just a series of inclined planes. Each hill is an inclined plane. A pulley system attaches to the coaster and pulls it to the top of the first hill. Then the pulley detaches. After that the coaster completes the ride on its own. A roller coaster works by changing potential energy to kinetic energy. At the top of the first hill the coaster has a lot of potential energy. The higher it is lifted, the more potential energy it has.

Gravity pulls the coaster down the hill. Once it starts moving downhill, it loses potential energy. That energy is changed to kinetic energy. The faster its speed going down the hill, the more kinetic energy it has. This kinetic energy carries it to the top of the second, smaller hill. As it goes up the second hill, the coaster gains potential energy. The change of energy repeats for each hill. Also the coaster's inertia tends to keep the coaster moving once it starts down the first hill.

Different kinds of wheels help make your ride smoother. The coaster is guided along the track by running wheels. Friction wheels keep the coaster from moving too much from side to side. Finally, brakes create enough friction to stop the coaster as the ride ends.

Glossary

compound machine machine made of two or more simple machines

distance how far something moves

efficiency amount of work a machine does compared to the amount of energy put into using the machine

effort force applied to a simple machine

energy ability to do work

force a push or pull

friction force caused by one object rubbing against another

fulcrum point around which a lever pivots or turns

gravity force that pulls objects toward the center of Earth

inclined plane simple machine that is a flat surface with one end higher than the other

inertia tendency of a moving object to stay in motion or a resting object to stay still

joule unit used to measure work

kinetic energy energy of motion

lever simple machine that is a rigid bar that turns around a fixed point

machine any tool that makes it easier to do work

motion change of position or place; movement

newton unit used to measure force

potential energy stored energy

pulley kind of wheel with a groove for a rope or cable

resistance force exerted by something you are trying to move

screw simple machine that is an inclined plane wrapped around a rod

simple machine machine with few or no moving parts that makes it easier to do work. The six types of simple machines are the lever, pulley, wheel and axle, inclined plane, wedge, and screw.

speed how far an object moves in a certain amount of time

wedge simple machine that is a type of inclined plane with one or two sloping surfaces

wheel and axle simple machine that consists of a large wheel fixed to a smaller wheel or shaft called the axle

work result of a force moving an object over a distance